THE HASTINGS SERIES

Fundraising Events Success Top Tips

Valuable Lessons from an Old-Dog Fundraiser

Ewan Hastings MInstF(Dip)

www.positivefundraising.yolasite.com

Text Copyright © 2016   Ewan C. Hastings

All Rights Reserved

ISBN-13: 978-1540725783

ISBN-10: 1540725782

Cover Photo Credit: Nadin Dunningan Photography Ltd

To all my fellow fundraisers, event guests, participants and competitors, and line managers who I have learned from or who made me realise what I needed to do in my fundraising to Make It Happen.

About the Author

Ewan Hastings has worked as a full-time fundraiser for nine UK charities, both large and small, in a fundraising career spanning over 22 years. He has run fundraising events right throughout that time. He loves passing on his fundraising knowledge, gleaned throughout his career, to help you on the road to success.

He was formerly a committee member of The Institute of Fundraising's Scottish Trusts, Foundations and Statutory Special Interest Group. He has also sat on the committee, and been Chair, of the Institute of Fundraising's Scottish Corporate Special Interest Group.

Ewan has spoken at the National Fundraising Convention and other fundraising conferences organised by The Institute of Fundraising and Professional Fundraising Magazine on various aspects of fundraising including raising funds from events, and has also written articles for a number of fundraising websites.

He currently works as the Trusts and Corporate Fundraiser for Waverley Care in Edinburgh, Scotland.

He has two grown-up children and lives with his wife just south of Edinburgh.

INTRODUCTION

I will never forget a late afternoon at work many years ago, not long after I started working as a community fundraiser for a large, national UK charity. My line manager had repeatedly said to me over the previous 2-3 months that I should get on and organise the charity's large-scale team fundraising event. Being young and naive, I ignored her (your first tip: don't ignore your boss when it comes to running fundraising events!) and carried on organising my first event for the charity.

A few weeks later, I felt pleased enough with how my first event had gone for the charity, to fully turn my attention to organising the team event. I read through an organisation manual to the event and, to my horror, realised that I had done virtually nothing to organise what was a massive event. Scarier still, I had just eight weeks remaining before the event was due to happen. Worst of all, I still had to sign up 20 teams of ten people to participate!

In the following eight weeks, I didn't see my wife, children, parents and friends as I worked 12 hours a day and most weekends to get the event organised. It was horrible; but I just got away with it. The event happened, with over 20 teams there, but there were some distinctly loose ends. It was a salutary lesson for me to learn that I had to be organised with running events and to leave plenty of time to organise them. On a positive note, it did show me what hard work and a steely determination could get me.

Since that time I have gone on to organise two formal Balls, dinner-dances, foreign treks, white water raft races, corporate fundraising events, sleep-outs, craft fairs and musical evenings amongst many, many other events.

I don't want you to go through what I had to with that large team event, which is why this book, although small, will help you fine-tune your event fundraising skills, build on your strengths and create more successful events for your charity. If you are new to raising funds through charity events, this book will supercharge your knowledge. Think of it as a practical manual for fundraising success, ready to take you to a higher plane of knowledge. From whichever angle you're approaching this book; you'll find it a fantastic resource to mastering the intricacies of securing funds through fundraising events.

In these pages is a collection of many hints and tips for everything to do with raising funds from charity fundraising events that have proven effective over the years, not just for me, but for many other old-dog fundraisers out there. Each one has been condensed to make this one of the easiest and quickest books to read on events fundraising ever! The more you consistently use these ideas the better they'll work for you.

As you look through these tips remember that fundraising and health and safety legislation changes constantly. Keep yourself abreast of the changes. You will also need to follow the rules and regulations of [The Fundraising Regulator](#) or [OSCR](#) if you work in the UK; or your own country's professional membership organisation or charity regulator for fundraising. Also, be aware of any local and national charity laws you need to follow.

I wish you all the success in your fundraising events as you seek to fine tune your fundraising. Organised well, fundraising events can become a successful keystone of your charity's annual fundraising.

I truly wish I'd had a book like this when I started off organising fundraising events all these years ago. It would have saved me a lot of time and effort!

Ewan Hastings MInstF(Dip)

Table of Contents

CHAPTER 1
GET THE BASICS RIGHT

CHAPTER 2
TEAM EVENTS

CHAPTER 3
GETTING ORGANISED FOR GOOD EVENTS FUNDRAISING

CHAPTER 4
FORMAL BALLS AND DINNER DANCES

CHAPTER 5
GETTING THE MOST OUT OF FUNDRAISING COMMITTEES

CHAPTER 6
GETTING CELEBRITIES INVOLVED IN YOUR EVENTS

CHAPTER 7
CORPORATE SPONSORSHIP

CHAPTER 8
THE TOP TEN WAYS TO PROMOTE YOUR EVENT

CHAPTER 9
EVENT VOLUNTEERS

CHAPTER 10
HANDLING MONEY AT EVENTS

CHAPTER 11
AFTER THE EVENT

CHAPTER 12
MISCELLANEOUS EVENTS TIPS

CHAPTER 13
INCREASING AN EVENT'S INCOME

CHAPTER 14
AND FINALLY...

Fundraising Events Success Top Tips

CHAPTER 1

GET THE BASICS RIGHT

- It is wise to give yourself at least six months, to a year, before a large event to properly organise it.

- You want to, ideally, have fundraising income ratios of 1:3 or more from your event. Thus for every £1/$1 you spend, you want to raise £3/$3, or more, in income. Some charities work on a 1:4 ratio.

- It's vitally important to keep everyone informed of an event's progress, so changes can be made in its organisation, if required. You might not see everything needing done.

- If someone asks you how many people are signed up to do an event, tell them **exactly** how many people have already signed and paid up, to do the event. Do not count those who are "thinking" of doing it, as, in my experience, these people or teams often do not go on to participate.

- Does a big event look daunting at the start? Take yourself miles forward in its organisation by doing lots of the smaller tasks that need done over the course of a single day or couple of days.

- I have found over the years that often emails do not work. Actually speaking with people over the phone is far more effective in getting people and teams signed up or in helping you with your event. Do not rely on an email. The maxim here is: <u>do it now, don't delay.</u>

CHAPTER 2
TEAM EVENTS

- It's tough getting corporate teams for events. A lot of the time it just takes hard graft. Getting on the phone and calling companies takes guts and perseverance to get to the right person to speak to. Getting two meetings might take you 30 calls. You can do these calls in two hours if you stick at it. Give yourself a treat at the end of making the calls.

- Approach a local, friendly recruitment agency to ask them if they can send your corporate team event challenge publicity directly to the HR department of hundreds of local companies for free. They can send it as a part of their next emailing or via their Facebook, Twitter or LinkedIn pages.

- Some charities are still using fax advertising to sign up corporate teams for challenge events.

- Facebook advertising on team events allows you to directly focus events adverts to people interested in doing your charity's events.

- Try promoting a team event the old-fashioned way: Get some event posters or leaflets designed and printed. Then walk around businesses in your area. Hand over the posters / leaflets to each company's receptionist, get them excited about the event, and ask them to stick your poster up on the office's staff notice board. By the time you get back to the office you may well have some calls or e-mails waiting for you asking for more information.

- To encourage people or a team to do an event, give them just two weeks to sign up. This tends to focus their minds. Get immediately on with contacting and signing up other groups. There should always be a constant moving forward with an event. If a group, you have previously contacted, signs up to do an event a few days or weeks later, then great. If not, you haven't wasted valuable time wondering when and if they'll participate.

- A good way to monitor the progress of a team and where you are with them is to create an MS Excel spreadsheet with columns noting dates when initial contact is made, information pack sent out, two week sign up date, date signed up, t-shirts sent out, sponsorship raised, thank you letter sent etc. *Download an example of one on my website (URL shown near the front and back pages).*

CHAPTER 3

GETTING ORGANISED FOR GOOD EVENTS FUNDRAISING

- It's a very good idea to spend some time formulating the perfect 100 word description of what your event actually is, close to the start of organising it. It'll be used time and time again in emails, letters, press releases etc., where you can simply insert the paragraph into whatever you are writing.

- A Frequently Asked Questions (FAQ's) sheet, given to event participants when they register for an event, can save you a huge amount of time in fielding phone calls, answering emails and social media messages from teams and individuals.

- Make sure you enter all event details into your charity's CRM system if you have one. Ensure all entries are correct when inputted to save time correcting later.

- An Event Forward Planner makes it so much easier to plan and organise an event. It will also keep you on track. In MS Word, open a new document. In Page Layout, under "orientation", select "landscape". Insert a table, four columns wide with at least 20 rows. Head up the columns "Task", "By", "Who" and "Comments". "Tasks" - Take time to think of all the tasks that you need to do on each separate line. "By" – what's the latest date that the task needs to be done by? "Who" – who is the person assigned to do the task? Will it be you or someone else? "Comments" – a status update on where you are with the task, always kept up to date. *Download an example of one on my website (URL shown near the front and back pages).*

- If you are producing tickets for your event, number them. Let's say you have a maximum of 140 spaces at your event. Number them 1-140. Get a sheet and place all the numbers against the names and contact details of the person who has bought the tickets. Be especially careful as your event heads to being a sell-out: stop online sales and make sales by telephone only, on a first-come-first-served basis. My advice to you would be that when you get to the last 20 tickets, take back control of the ticketing if you have assigned it to someone else. Decide on just one method of selling the remaining tickets: in person, online, by post. That way you will not lose control of the ticketing and not have "extra" people turning up to the event.

CHAPTER 4

FORMAL BALLS AND DINNER DANCES

(I refer to both Formal Balls and Dinner Dances as "Balls" below.)

- You should generally not have to pay for room hire at a venue. Hotels and other venues make plenty of profit from food and drink. Negotiate on the price with the sales or banqueting manager.

- Music: If you want your Ball to become an annual event I would strongly recommend getting a good live band to play at your first Ball as this will make the Ball much more appealing to prospective guests. Get recommendations from local people for the best bands. People will often buy a table on the strength of who the band are, and will come back again to the second year of the Ball if they are good.

- Do not give the venue your table plan until the morning of the event. This allows you to easily correct any mistakes and add or remove any tables or guests at the last minute as, I guarantee, there will be last minute changes!

- Table seating plans must be enlarged and clearly placed in the drinks reception room and beside the doors of the main venue. The more table plans there are to view, the better. They must always be placed where there is good light, so people with a visual impairment can see them clearly. This exercise is all about getting people seated quickly and the evening proceeding to schedule.

- Want to get people sat down quickly prior to dinner? Place a bagpiper, or a player of another loud musical instrument, at the back of the drinks reception to start playing as soon as dinner is announced. They play loudly whilst stepping forward every few bars of music to usher them into your main venue very quickly.

- Get the evening off to a good start by playing "Heads & Tails": Your compere asks everyone to stand up at the very start of the main part of the evening. They ask everyone to either put their hands on their heads (Heads side of the coin) or their backsides (Tails side of the coin). They then spin a coin. Depending on what side is revealed, all those with their hands on their heads, or backsides, have to sit down. Eventually, after a few spins of the coin you will end up with two people. The winner gets a prize: the Ball has an immediate atmosphere.

Making Additional Money at the Ball

- Coin Toss: Tossing coins at a bottle of alcohol on the dance floor during the band's break is a great idea to make extra money. Mark out three "lanes" on the dance floor and place a bottle of spirits / wine, or another prize, at the end of each lane. People toss a coin e.g. 50p piece at the bottle or prize. The closest coin to the bottle or prize wins that prize. You keep all the other coins. (Hint: get a cash float organised beforehand, so people can get change.)

- Lemon Bowling: Same format as above but people bowl three lemons for £1/$1/€1 at bottles or prizes lined, in three lanes, up at the other end of the dance floor. The lemons go everywhere but straight! Get your compere to commentate on the action. Closest lemon to the prize wins. I guarantee you'll have a big queue of people wanting to bowl and everyone will be in stitches, laughing at the funny antics on the floor.

- Raffle: Get some good prizes donated and assign volunteers to go round the tables selling tickets, in between courses and after dinner.

- Auction: Get your compere, or a local auctioneer, to run this for you on the evening. Get no more than seven quality auction lots. If you are struggling to get quality auction items, combine prizes to create a quality lot e.g. a) a chauffeur drive from someone's home to collect 4 four people to get taken to their b) local golf course for 18 holes of golf and c) lunch afterwards in a local restaurant, before being driven home. When confirming auction prizes for an event check out any terms and conditions that come with the prize and mention them in the advertising of the auction at your event. With auction prizes it is worth stating that "no refunds will be given" and "terms and conditions [if given] cannot be changed", to cut back on administration following the Ball.

- There are many companies now offering online, silent auction and raffle facilities using apps and table consoles, which simplify the whole process. Funds raised can be accelerated, as bids can be placed prior to an event as well as at the event too. Ensure you know the exact cost of these systems before you sign up for them, as they can be pricey and eat into the profit made from your event.

- Tombola: Can run right throughout the Ball. Peeks of Bournemouth sell pre-printed Tombola Tickets which makes the whole exercise very easy to organise. Assign at least two of your committee to get prizes.

- Silent Auction: Get some quality prizes donated. Create sheets for each auction lot and detail the "lot" at the top of the sheet, along with a photo of the lot if it is not on display. Below, have three columns for people to write their bid amount, name and telephone number. Put the sheets on a table next to its respective lot item. Have plenty of pens available for people to write their bids. I suggest having no more than 10 auction lots, as more tends to dilute the bid amounts. Note tips above under "Auction" re: terms and conditions and not offering refunds.

CHAPTER 5

GETTING THE MOST OUT OF FUNDRAISING COMMITTEES

- An ideal number for a Ball committee, in my experience, is 6-8 people. You don't want people on your committee with not enough (or too much) to do.

- Get an event committee together by contacting donors who have fundraised for you over the past few years. Also send out a short press release to your local media promoting the fact you are putting together a committee "for people who like to organise events for family and friends and who want to take it to the next level". You'll be amazed how many people like that, are out there!

- In approaching prospective committee members it is very important to say to them that committee meetings will not last longer than an hour and half at a maximum.

- If you can't run committee meetings during the working day, I would recommend starting them between 5.30pm – 6pm and finishing no later than 1½ hours thereafter.

- Frequency of committee meetings: if your event is a long time away, one meeting a month is fine. Have more frequent meetings the closer to an event date.

- Keep committee members up to date with event news e.g. number of tables sold etc. They must hear any event news before any members of the public.

- Need some more committee members to join your committee? Ask the existing committee members to each recruit another committee member. Double the effect for half the effort!

- There is no problem with asking each of your organising committee to be personally responsible in signing up at least three teams or sell three tables. With six committee members that could be 18 tables or teams!

CHAPTER 6

GETTING CELEBRITIES INVOLVED IN YOUR EVENT

- The website www.spotlight.com is the UK's leading celebrity resource with unrivalled celebrity knowledge and contacts. Use it to contact celebrities through their agents.

- Do everything you can to make a celebrity's agent respond to you in the easiest way possible, such as using "Yes / No" radio (option) buttons on your email.

- I have often found that a celebrity's email address is often the first name of the main one listed on their website. For example, info@georgeclooney.com might go to George's agent, where george@georgeclooney.com would go directly to George*.

- Celebrities don't have to be well known to be "famous". In the UK, Cillit Bang's "Barry Scott" – actor Neil Burgess – is a prime example of this. So think creatively on who you ask.

- I have never paid for celebrities to attend an event. I have paid travelling and / or accommodation costs. Most celebrities give their time for free.

- Always give your celebrity a small gift to take away for donating their time, such as a nice bottle of wine.

*This is just a hypothetical example!

CHAPTER 7

CORPORATE SPONSORSHIP

- Corporate sponsorship allows you to make more money through an event by, ideally, getting all the event's costs covered by the sponsorship.

- What to put in a simple corporate sponsorship pack:

   1. Cover Page: Your charity logo, the logo of the company you are approaching, your charity number and title of the corporate sponsorship opportunity.

   2. Introduction to the Opportunity i.e. what's in it for them.

   3. Introduction to the Charity.

   4. The Opportunity: List all the benefits of being a sponsor with the costs or costs of being a sponsor (see below).

5. Promotion Timeline: a sheet showing a timeline for all your promotion, media etc.

  6. Contact details: Who to contact and by when.

- Put your corporate sponsorship package in a report file. This creates a good impression of your sponsorship opportunity to the company or companies.

- In a time of recession, a big sponsorship ask can be cut down to smaller, more manageable asks e.g. a single company sponsorship of £10,000 or $10,000 can become ten individual company sponsorships of £1,000 or $1,000 each.

- Look at how other charities and companies do corporate sponsorship with their stakeholders. Learn what works for them.

- In the UK, corporate sponsorship can be subject to Value Added Tax (VAT). Check occasionally with HMRC as VAT rules can change.

- Do you have a friendly business contact or friend of the charity who you could ask to could circulate your sponsorship package around their networks and encourage sign-ups? They hand or send out the sponsorship packs to their business contacts. You deal with all the administration.

- Try to persuade your corporate sponsor to commit to sponsoring your event for three to five years, rather than one year.

- Ask your contacts on LinkedIn to set up meetings for you with prospective business people or companies who may sponsor the event.

Pleasing your Sponsor:

Event publicity: Put sponsor in posters; annual reports; invitations; on tickets; any event advertisements.

Signage: At sponsored event; at company's location.

Event Tie-ins: A mention in, and free advert, in event programme; promote company's products at event on a table; give company's product to event participants.

Logo and placement of the message: In press releases; annual reports; newsletters and e-newsletters; flyers and brochures.

Allowing company representatives at the event: Doing welcome at event; introduction of special guests; press conferences; presenting awards; cutting ribbons; complimentary team place or individual places in event for their staff or their guests; kick off events; helping to announce charity's new services at event.

<u>Promoting the company's products:</u> put company's product/s in goodie bag for participants to take away; promote product/s at your charity

CHAPTER 8

THE TOP TEN WAYS TO PROMOTE YOUR EVENT

N.B. It's very useful to develop a list of all the below that you can bring out for each event that you organise, so that all bases are covered for each of the events that you run.

1. Facebook advertising: Allows you to micro-target a specific event type e.g. runners, dancers, people who like participating in charity events etc., in your area, for a small cost.

2. Get event posters or flyers printed and drop them into local libraries, shops, pubs, clubs, churches, sports clubs, schools, sports centres, health clubs.

3. Write a press release about your event and send it to your local media. Most importantly, try and create a press photoshoot to launch your event

that has a very visual theme, or story hook, in order to entice press photographers to come along to the launch.

4. Make it possible for people to book online. Online booking is a prerequisite these days. People expect it. There are websites out there that charge very small administration fees

5. Ask everyone you know to promote your event – donors, supporters, service users, colleagues, friends, family and business contacts.

6. A lot of newspapers reduce their advertising rates close to their printing time or printing day. Phone their advertising department and haggle. I have often got large, quarter page adverts for events for just £100 (c$140). Once a paper's ad sales person gets used to you spending a smaller amount they'll call you when something becomes available at that price.

7. Make a list of all local and national "What's On" websites and ensure your event is listed on them all. Virtually all these websites allow you to submit your event information for free. The longer you can upload your event to them the better. Bookmark all the websites in a folder for easy access next time.

8. I have found that Balls / Dinners sell best through adverts in local lifestyle magazines. Again, haggle on the price of these.

9. Make sure that you put a video or some really good photos, demonstrating your event in action, on your website or social media posts (see the front photo of this book for a classic example of this!) Use photos throughout your publicity to personalise your event and attract more attention.

10. Really, really think who exactly the target market is for your event. Is it companies? Wealthy people? General members of the public? People getting married? Couples? People who have been affected by a particular medical condition? Then promote exactly to that sector. For example if it is runners for a local running event, think where they look at or go: running event websites, local lifestyle magazines, specialist running shoe shops, local gyms etc.

CHAPTER 9
EVENT VOLUNTEERS

- Make sure event volunteers are clearly briefed before an event. There was a classic mistake a few years ago at a 10K run, when a poorly briefed steward sent thousands of runners up the wrong street at a junction!

- There is no magic formula for getting event volunteers. Try a combination of the following: word of mouth; advert in local papers and websites; recruitment roadshows; local volunteer agencies; adverts up in local shops; Facebook advertising; use volunteers to recruit other volunteers; through local companies; in donor communications; do a media campaign.

- Always ensure you have enough volunteers at an event. Too few can be a problem.

- Consider hiring someone for a few weeks to get volunteers, if you have many volunteers to get, as it can be a time saver.

- Keep volunteers informed and updated on the event. This will make them feel more a part of something.

- Make sure all your volunteers are well watered and fed. Hungry and thirsty volunteers will definitely not come back.

- Contact all volunteers two weeks before an event. Send them a FAQ's sheet, detailing all information that they must know for the event and where and when they should meet you and your colleagues.

- ALWAYS enthusiastically thank volunteers following an event. Let them know how much has been raised through the event.

CHAPTER 10
HANDLING MONEY AT EVENTS

- Charity insurance companies often place conditions on the safe handling of money. Ensure you know what your charity's insurance company's conditions are and stick to them rigidly.

- Do not forget any cash floats required at your event. Organise them in plenty of time with your finance department or manager (I'd suggest at least two weeks in advance). Take plenty of change with you.

- Never announce a "total" raised from your event, at the event itself, unless you are 100% certain that the amount you announce is correct. Totals can often change in either direction a few days after an event, when some unexpected costs, or some more donations, come in. Announcing a wrong total can cause embarrassment to you and the charity.

- Assign someone to take control of all the money at your event. Ensure you know the arrangements for the safe handling of money following the event and when and where it should be safely deposited e.g. counted, bagged up and placed in a bank's night safe with the correct paperwork and key to open up the safe.

CHAPTER 11

AFTER THE EVENT

- Most charities announce the net amount raised from an event, rather than the gross amount, as this shows transparency of an event's costs to the event's participants and to the general public.

- A good way of stating a lower than expected total raised from an event is to announce "We have raised the handsome figure of £/$ from....".

- Give participants one month to get their online and offline sponsorship in from an event. Make it very clear before and at the event when their money is due in. Send out a reminder two weeks before the due date. After this date, send any stragglers an email mentioning that you "would now like to close the book on the event and announce a public total raised", giving them a further week to get you the money. At that stage announce a grand (net) total raised.

- A big event takes a year to plan. Book the following year's event as soon as that year's event has finished.

- You must thank everyone who has been involved in the event's success, however small their part, shortly after the event. A personally written thank you letter will reap dividends for you in getting them to help with future events – especially volunteers.

- Have a review meeting to discuss how to improve the event for next time. Stick a copy of the notes from the meeting in your event file, ready to refer to for next year's event.

- Can you apply the lessons learned from one event to use in other events you run? Events' fundraising is a constant leaning and improving process.

- Create an online questionnaire to distribute around your guests or participants asking them questions on their experience on the event. Have at least one, free-writing "Additional Comments" box. Learn from the lessons to improve the event in following years.

- Be realistic on your event's profit following an event, especially on a poorly performing event. It's better not running an event again if it has barely covered its costs. Cut your losses and get onto organising a different, more profitable event. Remember the *ideal* 1:3 fundraising ratio described above.

CHAPTER 12

MISCELLANEOUS EVENTS TIPS

- Long speeches at an event are a bore. Keep speeches short (2-3 minutes), to the point, and clear.

- Organising an event in its second year is much easier than the first year. However, do not let your guard down and keep your second event well organised.

- Income from an event should ALWAYS go up in its second year.

- Involve your service users and beneficiaries in an event and introduce them to the participants or guests to tell their own story. Very powerful!

- Make sure your event's location can cope with a massive influx of participants. One of the earliest events I organised was a white water raft race in deepest Perthshire in the Scottish Highlands, where I hadn't taken account of the effect of the increased traffic on the local, narrow roads, with hundreds of participants <u>and</u> their families and friends coming to the event. The event ran very late as a consequence.

- If you have the ability to set up a large scale event the day or evening before the event, do it. It really takes the pressure off on the day of the event.

- At very large events, I have found it useful to write cue cards, or set phone alarms, to remind me to do particular things at various times e.g. meeting the celeb, putting hot water urns on etc. Write or set them a few days before. Again, it really takes the pressure off on the day of the event.

- If you are responsible for an event, take FULL responsibility. Be visible, give clear instructions to staff or volunteers and keep a clear head. Never, ever drink alcohol at an event if you are in charge.

- Need an auctioneer for your event's auction? As well as antiques auctioneers, there are other auctioneers to approach – try livestock and car auctioneers who get asked to do charity auctions less frequently.

- It makes sense, as the event organiser, to wear bright clothing at an event, so people can find you quickly.

- If someone makes a complaint about your event, first and foremost apologise, even if it's not your fault. Try and sort out their complaint as quickly and as satisfactorily as possible. By doing so you'll dissolve the situation and can move on.

- Charged mobile / cell phones and walkie-talkies are very useful at events. There is no communication available to a dead battery.

- Buy an empty tool box and fill it with everything you think you might need at your event e.g. paper, pens, sticky tape, stapler, marker pens, hammer, screwdriver etc. This can be a lifesaver and be brought out again for each of your events.

CHAPTER 13
INCREASING AN EVENT'S INCOME

- Need to increase the total money raised from a team fundraising event in its second year and beyond? Tell the teams when they first sign up for the event, that there will be a cheque presentation ceremony towards the end of the event. It focuses the teams to raise more money as they won't want to embarrass themselves in front of the other teams. Give each team leader a large presentation cheque before the ceremony and get them to write the team total on the cheque before presenting it. Keep a tally of the cheque amounts as they are presented one by one, to cheers from other teams, and then simply announce the grand total raised at the event at the end! I started doing this with a large-scale team event in its second year and massively increased the income.

- Corporate sponsorship can help nullify some, or all, of an event's costs. Review the Corporate Sponsorship chapter.

- Can you reduce costs e.g. by order simpler food? Hire a cheaper band? Look at room hire costs? Do online ticketing only?

- Many other charities are making a lot of money from fundraising events. Pick a charity that you don't compete with, or who work in a different area to yours, and go and ask them what works for them. I did this with a Sleep Out event I ran for a charity I worked for, travelling to visit another city to speak to another homeless charity on how they ran their much bigger Sleep Out event. Learn from others.

- Listen to comments from people at an event and write them down. I once had a comment from a participant at an event, that we should take the event's moving candle ceremony and hold it as a separate event. We went on to run the "Candles in the Gardens" event in a city centre park in Edinburgh for years after, raising many more thousands of pounds for the charity in the process.

CHAPTER 14

AND FINALLY.......

Although you now have these tips, charity events fundraising can still seem an inexact science. My best advice to you is to just feel your way with each event you organise and apply the tips accordingly.

To find out more books in The Hastings Series and download free template documents to help you in your fundraising, go to www.positivefundraising.yolasite.com

On the Free Resources page put the following into the
password protect boxes to access the free resources:
Login: Top
Password: Tips

Connect with Ewan Hastings:
Email: toptips@gmx.com
LinkedIn:
https://uk.linkedin.com/in/ewanhastings
Twitter: @ScotFR

Text Copyright © 2016   Ewan C. Hastings

All Rights Reserved

FOR YOUR OWN NOTES OR TIPS

FOR YOUR OWN NOTES OR TIPS

www.ingramcontent.com/pod-product-compliance
Lightning Source LLC
Chambersburg PA
CBHW061223180526
45170CB00003B/1138